What on Earth? Tsunamis

What on Earth?

How many deaths?

How many people do you think have been killed by tsunamis in the last 15 years?

Turn this page to find out!

First published by 2005 by
Book House an imprint of
The Salariya Book Company
25 Marlborough Place
Brighton
BN1 1UB

Please visit The Salariya Book Company at: **www.salariya.com**

HB ISBN 1-905087-31-4
PB ISBN 1-905087-32-2

Visit our website at **www.book-house.co.uk**
for free electronic versions of:
You Wouldn't Want To Be An Egyptian Mummy!
You Wouldn't Want To Be A Roman Gladiator!
Avoid joining Shackleton's Polar Expedition!
You Wouldn't Want to Sail on a 19th Century Whaling Ship!

Due to the changing nature of internet links, The Salariya Book Company has
developed an online list of websites related to the subject of this book.
This site is updated regularly. Please use this link to access the list:
http://www.book-house.co.uk/WOE/tsunami

A catalogue record for this book is
available from the British Library.

Printed and bound in China.

Editors:	Ronald Coleman
	Sophie Izod
Senior Art Editor:	Carolyn Franklin
DTP Designer:	Mark Williams

Picture Credits Julian Baker & Janet Baker (J B
Illustrations): 6-7, 8, 9(t), 15, Nick Hewetson: 3, 9(b) The
Art Archive/Nasjonal Galleriet Oslo/Joseph Martin: 20,
Corbis: 12-13, Charles O'Rear/Corbis: 16-17, Lloyd
Cluff/Corbis: 18, Diego Lezama Orezzoli/Corbis: 19,
Stringer/Malaysia/Reuters/Corbis: 22, Reuters/Corbis: 25,
Empics/AP: 24, National Geographic/Getty: 10, Hulton
Archive/Getty: 21, AFP/Getty: 31, Getty Images News: 23,
eol.jsc.nasa.gov, ISS010-E-13079: 14, Daniel Heuclin,
NHPA: 26, NOAA: 11, NOAA: 29

Cover credits: Corbis, Stringer/Malaysia/Reuters/Corbis

What on Earth?

About 205,000!

Between the years 1990 and
2005, large tsunamis have
caused the deaths of around
205,000 people.

What on Earth? Tsunamis

DAVID AND HELEN ORME

Why are these waves so high?

Turn to page 6 to find out!

BOOK HOUSE

Contents

What on Earth? What is a seismologist?

A seismologist is a scientist who studies earthquakes.

Introduction

A tsunami is created when a very strong force disturbs an ocean. If you throw a stone into a pool, the stone takes over the space that was previously filled with water. The stone has pushed the water out. This movement of water disturbs the rest of the pool and produces a series of waves. When a huge disturbance occurs in a deep ocean, the same effect results but on a catastrophic scale. This is a tsunami.

Are tsunamis scary?

Yes! The effect of a tsunami can be devastating. Its waves can travel far inland causing great destruction. It is one of the most frightening natural disasters.

Do tsunamis happen often?

Yes. People think that tsunamis are rare, but this isn't true. Tsunamis are created in different ways and they happen quite often. However, a really big tsunami that causes huge amounts of damage and great loss of life is rare.

What is a tsunami?

A tsunami is a giant ocean wave, or series of waves that can travel for long distances towards land. These waves appear quite small in deep oceans and can race along almost **undetected**. Ships may not even notice them. However, as they near the shore these waves can become gigantic, rising more than 30 metres (98 feet) high, as they rush inland with enormous force.

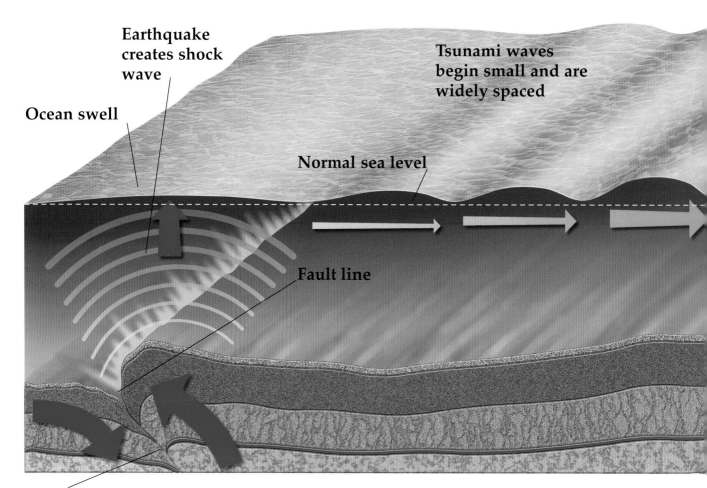

Earthquake creates shock wave

Ocean swell

Tsunami waves begin small and are widely spaced

Normal sea level

Fault line

Fault lines shift violently causing earthquake

A tsunami begins

In deep oceans powerful tsunamis can travel as fast as 700 kilometres (434 miles) per hour. The speed of tsunami waves depend on the depth of the water, so the deeper it is the faster the waves travel. Although travelling very fast, the waves are far apart and not noticeably high at this stage making them difficult to detect.

Tsunami grows higher and higher before it finally breaks

Coastline

Waves increase in height and get closer together

Where do tsunamis happen?

The Earth's surface is made up of **enormous** sections called tectonic plates. They rest on a vast layer of **hot rock** called the mantle. These plates are moving slowly at all times. Where the edges meet they either slide past each other, scrape together or crash head on. The area where plates meet is called a fault line.

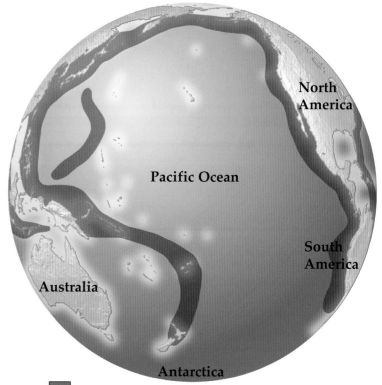

North America

Pacific Ocean

South America

Australia

Antarctica

Areas where tsunamis happen shown on maps

Can a coastline affect tsunamis?

In some places tsunami waves are affected by reefs and bays, or by the slope of a beach. When the wave hits, it can become even higher if it is forced into a narrow channel.

Do coasts change?

Earthquakes can cause major changes to the seabed and can affect ocean currents. The coast can be altered too. An earthquake can make a coastline drop, leaving it permanently under water.

Where are fault lines?

Fault lines are where earthquakes and volcanic eruptions are most likely to happen and are also the areas most affected by tsunamis. A major fault line stretching around the edges of the Pacific Ocean is often called 'The Pacific Ring of Fire'. Other fault lines can cause tsunamis in the Indian Ocean and off the coast of Africa.

Europe

Asia

Africa

South America

Indian Ocean

Atlantic Ocean

Antarctica

Fault lines

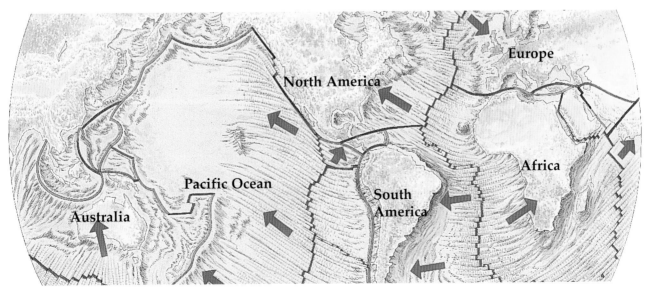

North America

Europe

Pacific Ocean

Africa

South America

Australia

Arrows show the movement of tectonic plates

Why do they happen?

A tsunami is created when an enormous force disturbs the ocean. The most common cause is an **underwater** earthquake. Earthquakes are measured using a special scale called the 'Richter scale'. Earthquakes measuring one or two on the Richter scale are too small for people to notice. But earthquakes measuring seven to nine on the Richter scale cause great devastation. However, a powerful earthquake at sea does not always cause a tsunami, everything depends on what happens on the seabed itself.

What else can cause a tsunami?

A volcano erupting can cause a tsunami. Tsunamis can be caused by landslides when a great mass of land falls into the sea, or when a great mass of ice breaks off from a glacier on the coast. A very rare cause would be an object from space falling into the sea.

What on Earth?

Shuddering planet!

Each day there are over a thousand earthquakes on our planet! Luckily, most of these tremors are too small to notice. There are about eighteen major earthquakes each year.

What is a tsunami like?

When a tsunami hits the shore, a wall of water crashes inland with **enormous** force. Within minutes everything in its path can be destroyed. There is often no sign of its approach so people are taken by surprise and do not have time to escape to safety.

Are the waves strong?

People, boats and entire villages can be **tossed** inland or swept out to sea. Tsunami waves can rip up forests and are strong enough to lift cars into trees and knock houses from their foundations.

Complete chaos?

A large tsunami can cause utter **chaos** leaving survivors with many difficulties to face. Landmarks will have disappeared and familiar surroundings may have changed beyond recognition.

As tsunami waves reach shallower water near land, they slow down. However, the tsunami's power now increases the height of the waves which also get closer together. What looked like a gentle ocean swell far out at sea has become a series of huge waves, rushing inland with frightening force.

What on Earth?

Danger danger!

In 1992, millions of turtles were killed when they were washed from their breeding grounds by a tsunami.

How do earthquakes cause tsunamis?

A tsunami can happen when one tectonic plate is forced underneath another on the seabed. This movement is slow and gradual and can go on for centuries. Eventually the strain on the upper plate becomes too much and it lurches violently upwards causing an earthquake. The vast amount of water pushed upwards by the earthquake can create a tsunami.

Where did an earthquake recently cause a tsunami?

On December 26th, 2004 a large earthquake occurred off the western coast of Sumatra in the Indian Ocean. The northwestern Sumatran coastline in particular suffered extensive damage and loss of life. This photograph (left) taken from space, shows the damage along the southwestern coast of Aceh Province, Indonesia. The brown areas were covered with lush, green vegetation before the tsunami hit the coast.

Tsunami damage, northwestern Sumatra (Indonesia)

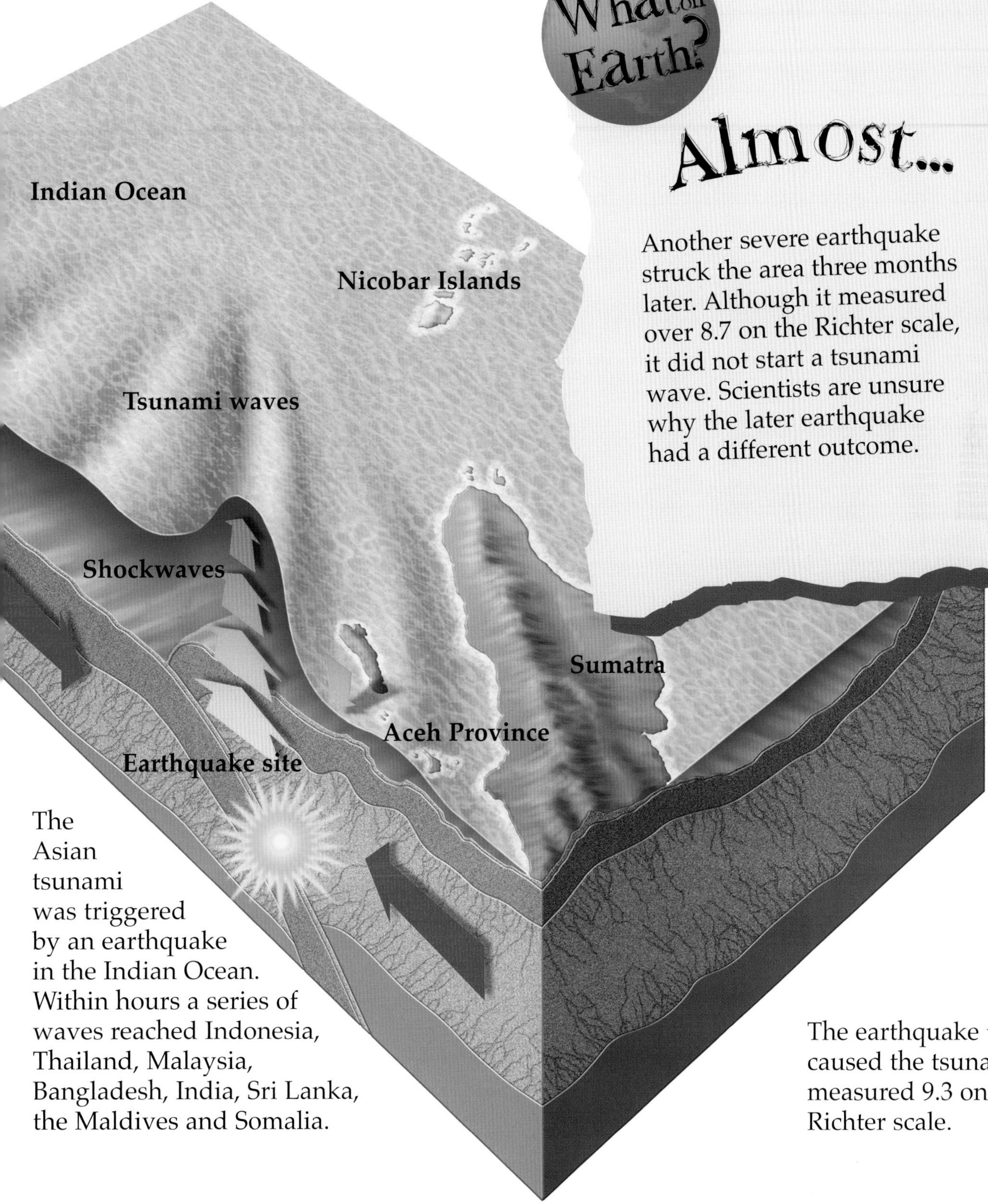

Indian Ocean

Nicobar Islands

Almost...

Another severe earthquake struck the area three months later. Although it measured over 8.7 on the Richter scale, it did not start a tsunami wave. Scientists are unsure why the later earthquake had a different outcome.

Tsunami waves

Shockwaves

Sumatra

Aceh Province

Earthquake site

The Asian tsunami was triggered by an earthquake in the Indian Ocean. Within hours a series of waves reached Indonesia, Thailand, Malaysia, Bangladesh, India, Sri Lanka, the Maldives and Somalia.

The earthquake that caused the tsunami measured 9.3 on the Richter scale.

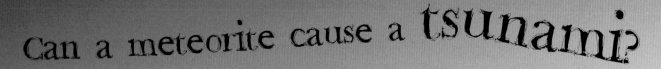

Can a meteorite cause a tsunami?

If a giant meteorite landed in the sea it would turn huge amounts of water into steam. As more water rushed in to replace it, a tsunami would be triggered. Fortunately, huge meteorites have not hit the Earth for a very long time, but scientists have found evidence of many hits in the past, on land and at sea.

What on Earth?

Can you believe it?

If a meteorite ten kilometres (6 miles) wide crashed into the sea, it would produce waves up to three kilometres (1.8 miles) high which would flood nearby continents.

The Barringer crater (below) in Arizona, USA was created by a meteorite

What is a mega tsunami?

The waves of a mega tsunami can be more than 100 metres (328 feet) high. They can cause enormous damage and kill many people. A mega tsunami can start like any other tsunami, but it usually takes something like a huge earthquake or landslide for it to become much more powerful.

The highest tsunami?

The highest tsunami recorded was in Alaska in 1958. It reached over 500 metres (1,640 feet) high because the waves were forced into a narrow bay. Luckily, only two people were killed.

Lituya Bay, Alaska

18

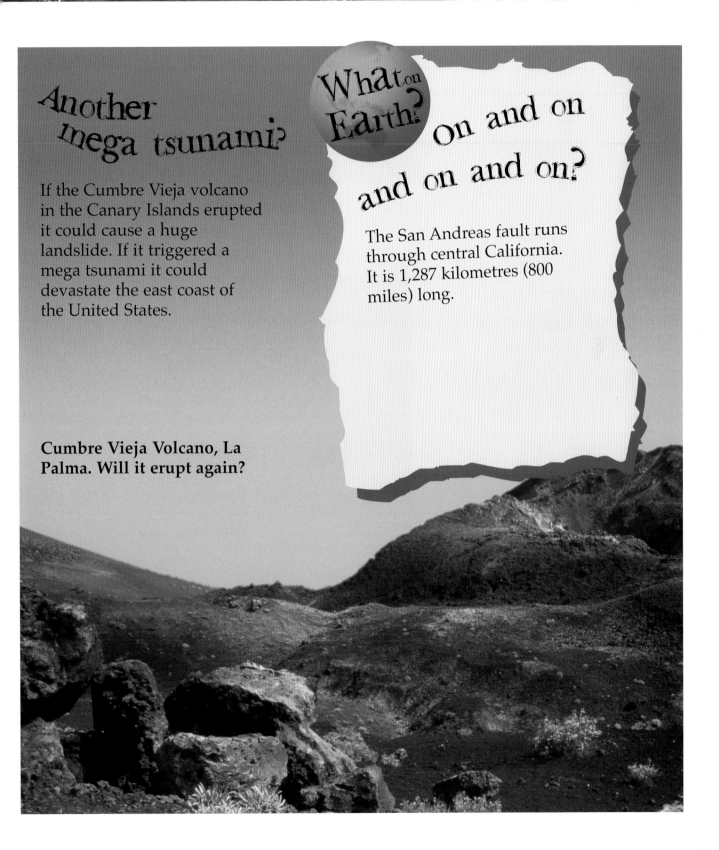

Another mega tsunami?

If the Cumbre Vieja volcano in the Canary Islands erupted it could cause a huge landslide. If it triggered a mega tsunami it could devastate the east coast of the United States.

Cumbre Vieja Volcano, La Palma. Will it erupt again?

What on Earth?

On and on and on and on?

The San Andreas fault runs through central California. It is 1,287 kilometres (800 miles) long.

Have there always been tsunamis?

Yes. Around 6000 BC an underwater landslide off the coast of Norway started a tsunami which hit the east coast of Scotland. And in 1755, tens of thousands of people were killed by a tsunami in Lisbon, Portugal. There was a famous volcanic eruption on Krakatoa in 1883 which caused a tsunami that killed 36,000 people.

Can a volcano change the colour of the sky?

The artist Edvard Munch painted 'The Scream' just after the Krakatoa eruption. It is thought that dust from the volcano caused the red sky that he painted.

Atlantis?

In 1650 BC the volcano on the Greek island of Santorini, erupted. It caused a tsunami wave between 100 and 150 metres (328 and 492 feet) high. Some people think this event started the legend of Atlantis.

The eruption of Krakatoa in Indonesia destroyed most of the island and created a series of waves that spread around the world.

Why was the Asian tsunami so deadly?

The Asian tsunami on December 26th 2004 is the worst to have happened in modern times. Although it was not as powerful as the Krakatoa tsunami, it was particularly devastating because of the huge loss of life – the greatest ever recorded. The tsunami hit in the middle of the morning during the busy holiday season.

Tsunami waves hit the shore

Run!

Large tsunamis are rare so people do not realise what is happening until it is too late. In the Asian tsunami, people came on to the beach to watch the approaching waves instead of escaping to higher ground.

Life after a tsunami?

Once it hits the shore a tsunami wave loses its energy quite quickly and the water drains back into the sea. However it leaves a devastated area which will take months, or even years to return to normal. The waves leave a vast amount of destruction and **debris** behind. As well as ruined buildings and roads, rescue workers have the difficult task of dealing with the bodies of people and animals killed by the tsunami.

An earthquake can make coastal levels drop. High tides can then flood the land turning it to salt marshes where crops cannot grow. Power and water supplies will be cut off and without fresh drinking water, people are at great risk of disease.

Fire?

Sometimes the most devastating effect of a tsunami can be fire, caused when gas pipes are severed and fuel tanks smashed.

How can science help?

Since the 1950s, tsunami warning systems have been set up around the Pacific Ocean. They are designed for high risk areas such as Japan and Hawaii. Satellites are now able to track tsunami waves and give more accurate warnings. Radio-operated buoys **detect** unusual waves, which can go unnoticed by ships and transmit warnings of danger to land.

How can mangroves help?

Scientists have worked out that mangrove trees could help reduce the force of a tsunami, but many have been cut down because of building developments.

How would you survive a tsunami?

Governments in Pacific countries are now looking at more early warning systems so they can predict earthquakes and tsunamis. Follow these simple rules and maybe you will be one of the lucky ones next time a tsunami strikes.

Tsunami Dangers

Flying debris can kill. Many of those killed by the Asian tsunami did not drown but were killed by pieces of wood and metal swept along by the wave.

Diseases like cholera, malaria and diarrhoea can quickly spread due to contaminated water after a tsunami.

Waves can rush towards the shore for several hours. This makes it difficult to rescue people trapped by the water.

What to do Check-list

Move quickly to **higher ground** or the top floor or **roof** of a building. Watch out for animals behaving oddly – they can detect a tsunami before humans. If you feel the shudder of an earthquake **head inland** – a tsunami may be coming. Listen out for **official warnings** and **expect more waves** – the next one may be bigger than the last. **Abandon all belongings**, this is no time to collect possesions and **don't count on your car** – the roads may be blocked!

As a tsumani approaches land, the sea may sweep far out from the shoreline. Don't stand and stare! It is about to crash back towards you along with the full might of the tsunami waves.

Tsunami facts

Tsunami is a Japanese word meaning harbour wave.

In one of the most destructive tsunamis to hit Hawaii, the waves began almost 3,700 kilometres (2,299 miles) away in Alaska's Aleutian Islands.

The Pacific Tsunami Warning Centre has issued 20 warnings since it was set up in 1949. Five turned out to be major tsunamis.

In the deepest oceans the wave speed of a tsunami can exceed 970 kilometres (602 miles) per hour. This is faster than a passenger jet.

Animals can show signs of panic and run for high ground before a tsunami reaches shore. This is why relatively few animals were killed in the Asian tsunami.

In the Asian tsunami, a girl's life was saved by the elephant she was riding on the beach. Just before the wave reached shore, it ran off to higher ground with the girl still on its back.

In Sri Lanka in 2004, a man survived by surfing in on the tsunami wave, ending up in his hotel restaurant.

Glossary

Atlantis A legendary island thought to have disappeared under the sea.

Buoy A float anchored to the seabed.

Crater A hole made by a meteorite when it hits the ground.

Debris Scattered remains like broken buildings and torn-up vegetation.

Fault lines Areas of Earth's surface where tectonic plates meet.

Glacier A large mass of ice.

Landslide Earth and rock which has fallen from a mountain or cliff.

Mangrove trees Trees with tall roots for support in swampy, coastal areas.

Mantle A vast layer of hot rock below Earth's surface.

Meteorite A piece of rock or metal falling to Earth from space.

Monitor To keep watch.

Ocean swell An ocean wave that does not break.

Reef A ridge of rocks or coral just below the surface of the sea.

Richter scale A scale that measures the power of an earthquake.

Salt marsh Area of coast that is regularly covered with sea water.

What do you know about tsunamis?

1 Does a tsunami change when it nears the coast?

2 Are survivors at risk from disease?

3 Which countries were hit by the Asian tsunami?

4 How could mangrove trees help?

5 Do satellites help to warn people?

6 What usually causes a tsunami?

7 Do earthquakes on land cause tsunamis?

8 Where does the word Tsunami come from?

9 Where did the 1883 tsunami start?

10 Is a tsunami just one huge wave?

Fishing boats, vehicles, and coastal houses (right) were wrecked when 10-metre-high (33 feet) waves hit the island of Okushiri. When did it happen?

Index

Pictures are shown in **bold** type.

Answers

1 The tsunami slows down but its waves get higher and closer. (See page 13)
2 Yes, because electricity and fresh water supplies are often badly disrupted. (See page 24)
3 Indonesia, Thailand, Malaysia, Bangladesh, India, Sri Lanka, Maldives & Somalia. (See page 15)
4 They could reduce the energy of the tsunami waves. (See page 26)
5 Yes, by tracking tsunamis as they cross oceans. (See page 26)
6 An undersea earthquake. (See page 10)
7 Yes, by triggering a landslide into the sea. (See page 10)
8 From Japan. It means 'harbour wave'. (See page 28)
9 Krakatoa, in Indonesia. (See page 20)
10 No, it is usually a series of waves. (See page 6)

In 1993, 240 people were killed when a tsunami hit the island of Okushiri. The wave started in the Sea of Japan.